Should the
GOVERNMENT
Pay for Health Care?

By Robert M. Hamilton

KidHaven
PUBLISHING

Published in 2020 by
KidHaven Publishing, an Imprint of Greenhaven Publishing, LLC
353 3rd Avenue
Suite 255
New York, NY 10010

Designer: Deanna Paternostro
Editor: Katie Kawa

Photo credits: Cover, pp. 11, 21 (inset, left) wavebreakmedia/Shutterstock.com; pp. 5 (top), 19 Erik McGregor/Pacific Press/LightRocket via Getty Images; p. 5 (bottom) Brooks Kraft LLC/Corbis via Getty Images; p. 7 (top) Universal History Archive/UIG via Getty Images; p. 7 (bottom) Jim Watson/AFP/Getty Images; p. 9 PTstock/Shutterstock.com; p. 13 Rungruedee/Shutterstock.com; p. 15 Monkey Business Images/Shutterstock.com; p. 17 Flamingo Images/Shutterstock.com; p. 18 (inset) Michel Passet/Shutterstock.com; p. 21 (notepad) ESB Professional/Shutterstock.com; p. 21 (markers) Kucher Serhii/Shutterstock.com; p. 21 (photo frame) FARBAI/iStock/Thinkstock; p. 21 (inset, middle-left) Gerry Boughan/Shutterstock.com; p. 21 (inset, middle-right) Ryan Rodrick Beiler/Shutterstock.com; p. 21 (inset, right) Dragon Images/Shutterstock.com.

Library of Congress Cataloging-in-Publication Data

Names: Hamilton, Robert M., 1987- author.
Title: Should the government pay for health care? / Robert M. Hamilton.
Description: New York : KidHaven Publishing, [2020] | Series: Points of view
    | Includes bibliographical references and index.
Identifiers: LCCN 2019002738 (print) | LCCN 2019005734 (ebook) | ISBN
    9781534567306 (eBook) | ISBN 9781534529977 (pbk. book) | ISBN
    9781534567252 (library bound book) | ISBN 9781534531222 (6 pack)
Subjects: LCSH: Medical care–Finance–Government policy–United
    States–Juvenile literature. | Medical care, Cost of–United
    States–Juvenile literature. | Health insurance–United States–Juvenile
    literature. | Health services accessibility–Economic aspects–United
    States–Juvenile literature.
Classification: LCC RA395.A3 (ebook) | LCC RA395.A3 H351185 2020 (print) |
    DDC 362.10973–dc23
LC record available at https://lccn.loc.gov/2019002738

Printed in the United States of America

CPSIA compliance information: Batch #BS19KL: For further information contact Greenhaven Publishing LLC, New York, New York at 1-844-317-7404.

Please visit our website, www.greenhavenpublishing.com. For a free color catalog of all our high-quality books, call toll free 1-844-317-7404 or fax 1-844-317-7405.

CONTENTS

Important but
EXPENSIVE

Health care is important! Seeing a doctor, going to the hospital, and taking medicine can help people stay healthy or feel better when they're sick or hurt. However, health care can also be expensive. In fact, some people don't get the health care they need because it costs too much money.

How can this problem be fixed? Some people believe the government should pay for health care for every citizen. Other people believe health care is a private issue and shouldn't be controlled by the government. Many Americans have strong feelings about health care, so it's important to understand this **debate**!

Many countries around the world have universal health care, which allows every citizen to get the health care they need without having to worry if they can afford it. The United States, however, doesn't have universal health care.

Medicare and
MEDICAID

The U.S. government doesn't pay for everyone's health care, but it does pay for health care services for some Americans through two **programs**: Medicare and Medicaid. Medicare pays for health care services for people 65 years old or older, as well as younger people with certain disabilities.

Medicaid pays for basic health care for people of all ages who don't make enough money to pay for it on their own. The number of Americans helped by Medicaid rose after President Barack Obama signed the Patient Protection and Affordable Care Act (PPACA)—also known as the Affordable Care Act (ACA)—into law in 2010.

Know the Facts!

In 1965, President Lyndon B. Johnson signed the bill that created Medicare and Medicaid into law.

One plan to have the government pay for health care for all U.S. citizens is called Medicare for All. As of late 2018, 70 percent of Americans thought Medicare for All was a good idea.

President Lyndon B. Johnson

MEDICARE for ALL
HEALTH CARE IS A RIGHT.

PAYING FOR IT?

How does the United States pay for Medicaid and Medicare? It requires its citizens to pay taxes, which the government uses for many services, including these two programs. If the government paid for health care for everyone, it would need more money. This means citizens would pay higher taxes.

Many people dislike the idea of paying more money in taxes. This is one of the biggest reasons why they argue against the government paying for health care. Some people believe if they're healthy, they shouldn't have to pay higher taxes to cover the cost of health care for people who are sick.

Know the Facts!

Canada has a system in which the government pays for its citizens' health care. In 2018, the average Canadian adult paid $4,640 in health care taxes.

Health care that's paid for by the government is most often **funded** by taxpayers. Some people would rather pay for health care on their own than pay higher taxes for a single-payer system.

Saving
MONEY

The United States is one of the only **developed** countries in the world without a universal health care system. This has led many people to compare the health care system in the United States to universal health care systems in other countries.

U.S. citizens pay more in health care costs than people from many other countries that have universal health care. Some people argue that if the government paid for health care in the United States, Americans would pay less in taxes than they pay now in health care costs.

Know the Facts!

In 2017, the average American adult paid $10,209 in health care costs. That's more than double the cost of health care in many other developed countries.

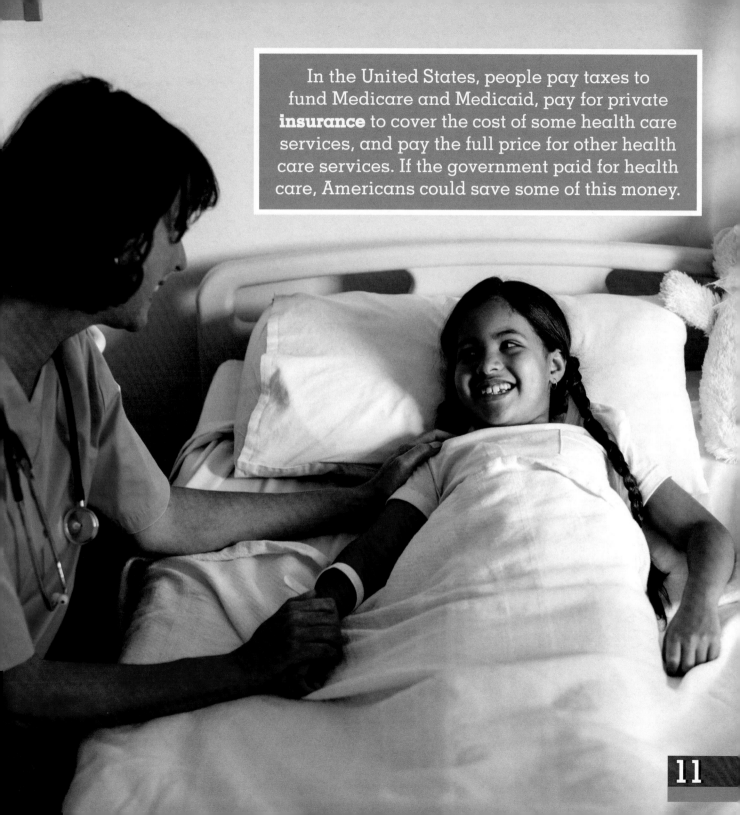

In the United States, people pay taxes to fund Medicare and Medicaid, pay for private **insurance** to cover the cost of some health care services, and pay the full price for other health care services. If the government paid for health care, Americans could save some of this money.

PATIENCE

Some people argue that the United States should be more like other countries that have universal health care systems funded by governments. Others, though, see that the health care systems in these countries aren't always good for **patients**.

If the government paid for everyone's health care, more people would go to doctors and hospitals because they could afford it. If the number of doctors stayed the same, this could lead to long waits before people receive the care they need. It could also lead to a lower quality of care as doctors and hospitals try to help more people.

Know the Facts!

A study of Canadian health care in 2018 showed that some Canadians had to wait longer than 45 weeks to get necessary **treatment** for a health problem.

People in countries around the world are working on plans to lower wait times for health care services. No matter who's paying for health care, it's important for people who are sick or hurt to be able to quickly see a doctor.

COUNTRY

Supporters of government-funded health care believe that even a long wait for health care is better than no **access** to health care at all, which is what many Americans are currently facing. They can't afford to pay for health care, so they often go without treatment they need.

This can lead to major health problems. **Experts** say it's one of the reasons why people in many other developed countries live longer than Americans. If the government paid for health care, every American would have access to important health care services without worrying about the cost. This could save lives!

Know the Facts!

As of late 2018, more than 27 million Americans don't have health insurance.

14

Some people believe the government should pay for health care because it would lead to a healthier country.

CHOOSE

Many people in the United States believe universal health care is a good thing. However, they also believe freedom is a good thing. Today, Americans can choose what they pay for health care—or if they have health care at all. Some Americans don't want that choice to be taken away.

People who oppose government-funded health care also worry about the government controlling what health care they can get. They believe the government might put limits on what health care services are paid for and what doctors people can see.

Know the Facts!

A 2017 study showed that 61 percent of Americans believe the amount they're being asked to pay for health care is fair.

Many doctors, drug companies, and others in the health care field are opposed to having the government pay for health care. They believe they'll make less money in a single-payer system than they make now.

HUMAN RIGHT?

Some people believe it's not the government's job to pay for health care. A growing number of people, however, believe that's exactly what a government should do to help its citizens.

The World Health Organization (WHO)—a group that works to make the world's population healthier—has called health care a basic human right. Many people think governments should do whatever they can to **protect** the rights of their citizens. In fact, more than half of all Americans believe it's the government's job to make sure every citizen has access to health care.

World Health Organization

Know the Facts!

The World Health Organization hopes to have universal health care for every person on Earth by 2030. It's working with governments around the world to make this possible.

Human rights are rights that all people have—no matter who they are or where they come from. If people believe health care is a human right, they're more likely to support government plans to pay for it.

The Debate
GOES ON

After learning the facts and arguments on both sides of this debate, do you think the government should pay for health care? People across the United States—from average citizens to government leaders—are asking themselves the same question. This debate has been going on for many years, and it shows no signs of ending soon.

The opinions people have on this issue **affect** the laws that are passed, the ways tax dollars are spent, and the ways people vote. This is why it's important to understand different points of view—not just yours!

Know the Facts!

In 2018, health care was the most important issue for voters in the United States.

Should the government pay for health care?

YES

- Americans pay too much money for health care.

- If the government paid for health care, more people would get the health care they need, and the country would be healthier.

- Health care is a human right, and the government's job is to protect the rights of its citizens.

NO

- If the government paid for health care, it would really be paid through higher taxes.

- More people would use health care services, and wait times for these services would go up.

- Too much government control takes away people's freedom.

The health care debate is important, and it's good to understand and respect people with different opinions on this issue. You can use a chart such as this one to make this debate easier to understand.

GLOSSARY

access: The ability to use or have something.

affect: To produce an effect on something.

debate: An argument or discussion about an issue, generally between two sides.

developed: Having many industries and few people who are unable to buy the things they need.

expert: Someone who has a special skill or knowledge.

fund: To provide money for a special purpose.

insurance: An agreement by which a person pays a company and the company promises to pay money for some or all health care costs.

patient: A person who receives care from a doctor.

program: A plan under which action may be taken toward a goal.

protect: To keep safe.

treatment: Care given to a person or animal that is sick.

For More
INFORMATION

WEBSITES

National Archives: Social Security Amendments (1965)
www.ourdocuments.gov/doc.php?flash=false&doc=99
The National Archives website describes the story behind the creation of Medicare and Medicaid.

World Health Organization: Universal Health Coverage
www.who.int/universal_health_coverage/infographics/en
This part of the World Health Organization's website features animated scenes that can help you better understand what universal health care is and why many people believe it's so important.

BOOKS

Biskup, Agnieszka. *Medical Marvels: The Next 100 Years of Medicine.* North Mankato, MN: Capstone Press, 2017.

Braun, Eric. *Taking Action to Improve People's Health.* Minneapolis, MN: Lerner Publications, 2017.

Higgins, Nadia. *US Government Through Infographics.* Minneapolis, MN: Lerner Publications, 2015.

Publisher's note to educators and parents: Our editors have carefully reviewed these websites to ensure that they are suitable for students. Many websites change frequently, however, and we cannot guarantee that a site's future contents will continue to meet our high standards of quality and educational value. Be advised that students should be closely supervised whenever they access the Internet.

INDEX